This book belongs to:

_____

Unique and Me

Marie Hinkle

5 Sail Publishing
Jacksonville, Florida

Copyright © 2020 Marie Hinkle
All rights reserved. No part of this book may be reproduced, stored in a retrieval system, or transmitted in any form or by any means, electronic, mechanical, photocopying, recording, or otherwise, without written permission from the publisher 5 Sail Publishing, 14286 Beach Blvd., Ste. 19-277, Jacksonville, FL 32250, or through the publisher's website, www.5SailPublishing.com.

Book and cover design by Sagaponack Books & Design
Illustrations by Afsaneh Bagherloo

ISBNs:
978-1-7341248-0-4 (softcover)
978-1-7341248-1-1 (hardcover)
978-1-7341248-2-8 (e-book)

Library of Congress Control Number: 2020904009

Summary: A child understands she is unique, and with education, mentors, and support of family and friends, she can be anything she wants to be—someone great.

JUV039140 Juvenile Fiction / Social Themes / Self-Esteem & Self-Reliance
JUV074000 Juvenile Fiction / Diversity & Multicultural
JUV006000 Juvenile Fiction / Business, Careers, Occupations
JUV035000 Juvenile Fiction / School & Education

5 Sail Publishing
Jacksonville, Florida

Printed and bound in the United States of America
First Edition

Acknowledgments

Thanks to my husband, who encouraged me to pursue a lifetime dream of mine to become an author. Since I became a mother, my children have inspired me with memorable adventures that have created special stories. Mrs. Guthrie, our school art teacher, gave me the push I needed to begin the work, and because I said it out loud, I had to complete the book.

This book is dedicated to my family.

"Nothing is impossible.
The word itself says
'I'm possible!'"
—Audrey Hepburn

Unique and Me

I am Mommy's dream come true.

I come from a blend of cultures. I come from a mix of colors and an array of languages too. Unique and me

I am clever enough to mold and create.
Unique and me

I come from a dash of independence and determination.
With a pinch of strong will.

I have 2 strong arms, 2 long legs, and a mouth full of teeth that light up any room when I smile big.

I have 10 delicate fingers, 10 cute toes, 2 eyes to see, and a small nose.

I have thick hair on my head.
I have a sensitive soul.
Unique and me

I am one of a kind, even with glasses, braces, and dimples so deep.
I am special and unique.

No one else has the same recipe as me. Freckles, moles, and hair on my toes.

This makes me unique.

It is up to me to build my future.
To be anything I want to be.
The ideas are endless and all mine to make.
Unique and me

Who will help me find my way?
On this roller-coaster path and windy road,
I will work tirelessly.

    Unique and me

I am destined to be someone great.
What will it be?
        Unique and me

Discussion Questions

1. What do you want to be when you grow up?

2. What are your personal goals?

3. What are your academic goals?

4. What traits do you need to achieve these goals?

5. How can these traits help you achieve these goals?

6. Who can help you achieve these goals?

7. How can you help others achieve their goals?

8. Why is it important to set goals?

9. What is success?

10. How will you know if you are successful?

ABOUT THE AUTHOR

Marie Hinkle is a seasoned educator who has had the opportunity to teach in several schools across the United States. Her greatest honor was being voted Teacher of the Year. Mrs. Hinkle is passionate about reading and empowering children. She lives in Florida with her husband, three kids, one cat, and a turtle. In her free time, she loves to travel and spend time with her family at the beach.

Learn more about Marie at 5sailpublishing.com.

www.ingramcontent.com/pod-product-compliance
Lightning Source LLC
Chambersburg PA
CBHW042029100526
44587CB00029B/4347